Dreamburgh, Pennsylvania

Dreamburgh, Pennsylvania

poems

Gregory Lawless

Dream Horse Press
Warrenton, Oregon

Dream Horse Press
Post Office Box 670, Warrenton, Oregon 97146

Dreamburgh, Pennsylvania Copyright © 2022
Gregory Lawless

Printed in the United States of America
Published in 2018 by Dream Horse Press

ISBN 978-1-935716-45-7

Cover artwork:

Autumn
by Yelena Panyukova

CONTENTS

I

Little Matter / 13
Toulouse / 15
The Griefs / 16
Little Matter / 17
The Awes / 19
Skating Rink / 20
Public Speaking / 21
Why I Almost Never Leave the House/ 22
Apples, Crosses / 23
Locker / 25
Little Matter / 26
The Whatnot / 27
Little Matter / 28
The Part of Summer That's Easy to Talk about / 30
Tuesday / 31
Little Matter / 32
On the Revolutions of the Heavenly Spheres / 33
Drift / 35

II

Pool / 39
It Just Looks Like I'm Dancing / 40
Forever-Voice / 42
Exchange of Territory / 44
Arcadia Groundskeepers Inc. / 45
Just You Wait / 46
Urban Theology / 48
The Animal / 49
Meditation on Outsourcing / 50
Warp Drive, or The Cabin Boy of Starfleet / 51
Silver / 53
Emergency / 55
Death Star 2 / 56
Note to Super Villain / 57

People Need to Talk Less on Planes / 59
Teeth Muse / 61
Getting Lost on the Back Roads of Pennsylvania, While Trying
    to Find His Parents' New House, the Author & His
    Now-Ex-Girlfriend Stop by the Side of the Road &
    Consider What to Do Next / 63
Little Matter / 67
Dear Things / 68
Crag / 69
Canteen / 70
Dreamburgh, Pennsylvania / 71

Notes / 73
Acknowledgments / 74

I

Little Matter

For Peter Richards

It should have been a planet
with peace and fog, with big piles
of water taking dictation
from the stars. It should have
cost nothing to get there.
It should have made you
want to give up candy
and think about working
for the government. It should have been
the kind of planet where animals
have sleeping contests
and the night sky like
a sliding board, and when
you're bored you recite something
you don't understand
in public, and people
hear it and do the same. It could have
been a republic of mystery, this
planet. We could infect

each other with wow. There might
be a river or two of blood.
There might be dying icicles.
Maybe some fall asleep
in this place, thinking of war
machines or new ways
to kill a spider, but
it could be a planet
where you don't run out
of ways to say I'm sorry

or take mine, I'm not
hungry, or there's plenty
more where that came from. It should be
someplace you can find
with a telescope or a poem,
and dream about
without getting hurt.

Toulouse

I beg the clematis to quit clawing the brick.
I beg my wife to take the washcloth from her eyes.
Itsy, itsy, itsy, says my daughter, for each
of my stitches. Once, on a staircase in Bruges,
begins a poem, once in a library
in Toulouse. I'm sick of arbors, those spears, like hairs
on a dream. In one dream, I'm so flummoxed
with awe at the sight of Mount Father
that my heart grows arrows and sails
and dissolves in the sea. You spend 2 percent
of your life waking up, .07 percent checking
your mouth for blood. You spend 8 percent
of your life wanting to talk about your dreams
but staring instead at potted ferns.
Does this foyer make you feel lonely? you ask aloud,
or is it just me? Just you
says your father, coughing up
pieces of cloud.

The Griefs

Oddly enough, you can only board them
in one spot: a little platform downtown
just past the bus station and laundromat
where the dark gray train rattles
fluff from the cottonwoods
in summer or spare rain from the maples
in April. The conductor lowers a metal
gangway ramp with a stomp and
it takes a long time to get on. The Griefs run
south and you carry your bags
in your lap. Everyone looks wet. You look
out the window for want
of something to do. If you have a problem
the conductor will come by
and listen to you, but only
for a mile or two.

Little Matter

Field trip-sized headache.

Ad for a cruise ship
that bops the arctic

in the puss. Little girl

getting her master's
in the pathetic fallacy.

Ad for a fork
with a flashlight attached

so you can eat
in the dark.

School play about
a log cabin where something

boring once happened.
Documentary about making

eye contact,

about answering-machine
tape. Student essay

called "I Hate

the Past" with a Works Cited page

a mile long. Two bullies
having a taunt contest.

One calls the other what
the other called the other.

Makes you want to give up
and paint wooden ducks

or smuggle model boats
into bottles

like a fart in a dream.
Imagine

a submarine the size
of the Azores carrying all

the Tom Clancy novels
that retired guys ever read

at their beach houses
in Maine. Now imagine

a Tom Clancy novel
about feelings and art.

When you're done
put the toilet seat down,

pull down the shades.
My lines are short

because they're afraid.

The Awes

Are tiny birds with little black raincoats
and drill-bit eyes and great patience

whose ideogram-shaped feet
which mean risible
& what-was-that? are perfect
for slapping fish
out of the river.

Their mouths are always open
through their silent-movie flight

over marshlands and canyons.

Li Po called them the dilations
which means the space between chess pieces
according to Li Po.

Legend has it, he only painted them
on horseback at night, his eyes closed.

And his paintings are widely considered
to be the worst of the ancient world.

Skating Rink

From one side of the rink
you can see the other side
frozen, curving, returning
like the past
you have to live through it
over and over again
before you get it right
and they let you out.
No wonder
children collapse
kicking their blades
in the air, reaching
their hands up
to snatch you
like a new father
no wonder
a nosebleed here
a rolled ankle there
something broken
you look down now
but you keep going.

Public Speaking

Make eye contact with your audience.

Take off your glasses, your shirt.

Show them your tattoos of hawthorns and tines of lightning
striking the grasslands.

Share an anecdote about miracle snowfall in the fourth century,
about abiding humanity in a war-torn country.

Read them your journals from your year at sea.

Everyone should spend a year at sea, you say, using yourself as
an example.

An example of what? someone shouts from the back.

See here, you say, pointing: The chandelier filled with electric
snow. The shivering crystal, we are all shivering crystal...

Someone coughs himself to sleep.

Shadows dash through the spotlight.

Do you remember? you say, thinking of something to say.

But it is quiet.

No one remembers.

Why I Almost Never Leave the House

I don't go downtown
anymore. And even if I do
I come back bored
and scared of what
I've bought. My car
can barely make it
down to Main Street
before it turns around
and shuffles back. It wants to tick
and drip in the dark
garage where all my tools
are sick. They won't come
out. The toolbox latch
is rusted shut. It's summer
now. I ought to pound
some seed into the lawn.
The grass has asthma.
It's brown and short.
The mail needs my help.
The bills are crying
out. My house is vague
and white, and I like it
from the inside, not
the out.

Apples, Crosses

The shirt is tired of having a man inside of it.

The pillow is tired of smelling like dreams.

Pass me the stopwatch. I want to time the paradigm shift.

Your painting is beautiful: apples, crosses, planes, and strangers.

I know so many strangers.

Once I saw a film about a samurai who fought the bomb in Nagasaki.

One time I saw a film about a hand of solitaire on a submarine.

Sometime between whenever and whenever.

Says the stopwatch.

What's the difference?

The man is tired of having a man inside of him.

Like a father with a miner's lamp.

And a tiny yellow mother. Whistling in a cage.

Here the samurai's sword is bright beneath the fires.

Here the sonar pangs of passing whales.

Dear you. Dear you. Dear you.

We've come so far together.

Says the captain. Through crackling speakers.

Strange, says the stranger.

We never met here before.

Locker

On the first day of September
you open the locker
and see inside some joker
from last year
has left a mirror there
with the word "loser"
written across your eyes
in black Magic Marker.
And seeing it now
makes it seem
suddenly inescapably
true, and
this witch doctor
of the soul
is probably watching you
somewhere out of sight,
cackling into his fist
or coat—but, of course,
he had to write the word
across his own face first,
so you look around
for him now,
whoever he is, who
answers to the same name
as you.

Little Matter

When I read Kafka's
Metamorphosis, I knew the whole point
was to throw apples

at your son
until he went away. At night I play

that chatterbox Rachmaninov
before the neighbors take to their balconies
with rugs and brooms

to beat away my sleep.
In an apartment building like this,

almost everything's revenge.
I know you didn't ask,

but all the flowers are fake.

The Whatnot

It's smallish, hard
to see. You can't quite
make out the edges
in this light, you can't
quite place the shape.
It's too heavy
to pick up,
but when you look
away it rolls away
under the table, or into some dark
corner behind the curtains,
the potted mums.
The cat doesn't
like it. You're wife wants you
to clean it up. You don't
talk about it
with your friends,
even when they point
and squint. Instead,
you just change
the subject. But you're always
changing the subject.

Little Matter

I come from a village of stonecutters
who knock two stones together
at night and find their way
by the sparks. No one wanted me
to leave the village, which is why
I left. When I return
to visit them now, I can't explain
that I haven't seen
the whole world, just two or three cities
I've known well enough
to want to leave
as well. They don't
believe I would abandon
them just to live a life
as small as theirs
somewhere far away. So I tell them
about the dragons
of Michigan and the great golden highway
connecting California
to Japan. I point
over their shoulders at places
like Asia and Atlantis,
a month's travel,
I lie, by mule. I never
mention flight, the most
disappointing wonder
of the outer world. And since
it's as much a mystery
to me as it is to them
I don't say why

I've come home. Instead, I clap
stones together
and follow my pile
of lightning through
the dark, stumbling
badly, as in days
of old.

The Part of Summer That's Easy to Talk about

They were hemlocks,
I think. The boy and his father
sawed away the sick
branches. That's what I saw
but I can't even say
what kind of trees
they were, so
you shouldn't listen
to me. I don't listen
to me either. On one branch,
a crow staggered
and lazily flicked its wings
to keep balance
until the father had
severed the last inch.
Then it flew to another
tree. You can't saw
down that crow, I thought,
and the boy caught
the branch below
and chewed it up
with his machine.

Tuesday

The woman across the street only yells
at her pets, the black Lab with the yellow
disks of cataracts and her three cats
that eat cans of gray turkey pâté between
screams on the front porch steps: Get in,
go out, come on. Whatever she says,
they don't. The cats lick the cut metal
lids and sweep their faces clean, just like
they must. Sometimes, I see inside
her house: the buckled linoleum
by the sink, drab paneling in the halls.
The living room so miserably
clean. She stacks her trash in tidy piles
outside on garbage day. Which sounds,
my wife says, like a kind of holiday. Or
like something you live though every day.

Little Matter

It was winter. I read the same book
on reincarnation a dozen times.
I felt like I should get a doctorate
in being alive
sent to me one day
in the mail. Then my wife and I
had a child. He was no heavier
than two bags of apples
but still the whole universe
was poured into his skull. Who were you
in your last life? I asked. I knew
he knew the answer
but couldn't say. And that one day
that fact would be replaced
with language, and he would live
the rest of his life
trying to get it back. I showed him
photographs of tundra
and the deserts
of central Asia, things
that would justify a long silence
if he chose. We spoke
in babble, that middle
ground of souls. And in the spring,
when he said his first word,
dripping in the bath, I pushed
his plastic submarine
under the water, then watched it
bob up again, pretending
I hadn't heard a thing.

On the Revolutions of the Heavenly Spheres

A precise V of geese and their immaculate
laugh track cruise north toward Canadian marsh

in the dark. My dream journal begins, *The billion-fired sky*
and ends
with a shopping list

of planets to see
before I wake, or die. Now

the spotlights from a monster-truck show
on the outside of town

swirl through the low clouds and icy constellations
like some ecstatic revision

of the principles of parallax
and retrograde motion. I can almost hear

the crunching steel and revving engines,
and I imagine

the titanic tires spinning

in mid-flight, the painted flames
and a thousand people

in the bleachers, cheering each crash
and collision, screaming

the mythic names, The Equalizer, King Krunch,
and The Carolina Crusher,
above the commotion—all of them

poised to rocket
out of their bodies
and burn a frothing, fiery arc

into heaven, while the geese
slice briefly through the spotlights,

casting their shadows toward
some distant and unknowable world.

Drift

In the desert
they found fossils
of my father
as a young man,
his Converse sneakers
dripping with tar, stacks
of old beer cans
and all of his hair.
One paleontologist
took pictures
of the whole dig team
packed into his wrecked
yellow Mustang,
with the scarred
fender and dented
doors. That was before
he learned to walk
upright and carry
a briefcase. Now his body
is held together
with a necktie
and mortgage,
and his offspring
have scattered
to climates
he cannot survive.
Still, we call him
once in a while
just to hear
his rough voice,

that prehistoric
grumble, like continents
cracking and drifting
apart, carrying some of us
this way, some
of us that.

II

I am a worthless boat.

Shakespeare

Pool

I was swimming laps in the pool, snorting and huffing through the water.

It was cold. I was tired.

I wanted to get out and show my shame to the birds.

But, anyway. I kept going.

My wife threw her cigarette into the pool. You're dying, she said.

The birds knew I was dying and stared down from the trees.

Hey, I said, thrusting my head out of the water.

I'm not dead yet.

I throbbed and kicked wildly, swinging my arms.

I've lived a good life, I thought, but, really, I hadn't.

Bubbles poured out of my nose like shreds of sky that didn't belong in the water.

My life didn't belong in the water either, but my death was another story.

Waxwings, grosbeaks, little finches in the trees.

My wife just stood there, shaking her head.

Watch this, I said.

Look at me go, I said.

It Just Looks Like I'm Dancing

You have me
in your tractor beam. When I try
to run away it just looks like I'm dancing
at gunpoint, or like someone
somehow is playing a joke
on my nervous system,
which is what it looks like
when I dance
anyway. I dig my heels
into the carpet. I grab onto a banister
or, foolishly,
a lamp. So I have this lamp
in my hands as I'm drawn
toward you on a slow
conveyor belt of awe. I should hit you
with the lamp and watch the light bulb
smash apart like a tiny sun
having a coronary embolism
but I can't because your tractor beam
makes my hands heavy
as dictionaries. If I could open them
now pressed leaves and flowers
would flutter to the floor
like the daydreams
of old science projects. Look up the word
"dictionary" and there is a picture
of my hands
full of light, crushed flowers
and words. But look up
"tractor beam"

and you'll see a picture of me
dancing apart
in your direction,
while you have your hands raised
like a bad
magician. And I don't know
if I'm headed
toward your embrace
or my destruction.
Or if the two of us
will crush together
in a single voice, a single
imagination.

Forever-Voice

I use it in libraries.

At the DMV.

Passing through customs after a month on the ocean.

On a tour of the Gulag.

It's a big hit at monasteries.

And I use it to plant little dreams in my mother.

Keep a garden, I say.

Call dad.

Take the cucumbers from your eyes.

Whenever you say, Where are you taking me? Forever.

What did the history teacher say to the eraser? Forever.

Darwin, on the Galápagos, counting turtle eggs:

Forever, forever, forever.

But no one can hear you.

Even now. No one is listening.

Bullshit, says mother.

I'm listening.

Exchange of Territory

I could not deem these Planetary forces
Annulled—
But suffered an Exchange of Territory—
Or World—

Emily Dickinson

Early one spring, in what was left of the spring, I came across a gas station by the river.

Inside there was a mirror, sashed with ash and fine scratches, and a little cot, and the nubs of candles burnt away on a crate.

I made myself at home, if this is ever the case.

With winter, I thought, I would have to topple the shack, and drag the wood to a cave, and burn it there, in order to sustain.

But in the meantime, I would dream.

I would shiver.

And look out at the wick-colored world through the surviving glass and wonder.

But what was there to wonder?

Arcadia Groundskeepers Inc.

What violence we do
to the landscape: shaving

the bushes down
to stumps; greasing

the bugs; plugging gopher holes
with lye. I mean,

have you ever seen
a perfect lawn?

You choke
on the green.

The sprinklers slap you
in the eyes.

Beautiful women come
out of the house

and tell you
to stop staring

or else.

Just You Wait

I'm lonely
for the word—a spare

world, a dream
of icicles,

for the charred

sparrows
nesting in mud.

I am glass stars
in the kiln. I am

a shout in the bones. Here

my hands chandelier
together. Here
they curtain apart.

I remember
your yesterday-fingers.

Your satellite earrings
pulsing at night. Do you remember

what they called it
here before they built

it: the Unbuilding? The Just-

You-Wait? Months from now
this space
will be a staircase

and this will be the voice
you hear

when the boards

start creaking
in the dark.

Urban Theology

For George Scala

I run into the courtyard with a broom
to scare the angels. They're eating

bread crumbs and hotdog buns
from the ground and stealing

quarters from the fountain.
They flock from one tree

to the next as I wave my broom
around like a flag. They have dark

eyes and their wings are scarred.
They bite each other and me

with tiny mouths. In another ten million
years their teeth will fall out. But today

is today. Their halos burn
away the leaves of the Norway

maples and singe the broom's
whiskers. Their droppings clog

the grates. Poor things, the angels,
bored to death by everything

they understand. Tell them a joke,
and they fall asleep,

weeping. They know every punch line
ever known to man.

The Animal

All my life I wanted a wild animal.

The only problem is: they're wild.

So it seemed like a bad idea, at first, to bring the animal home.

Here he is.

It's not fur exactly. They're more nails than claws.

He doesn't let you see his eyes.

His only mood is wildness.

Sometimes when I set a lard pail full of crabapples and dead birds before the guest room door, he lets me feel his hair.

But there's no us in our touch.

Still.

We get along somehow.

The animal has everything he needs, except for the fact that he lives with me in this small suburban house.

We're too used to things to change them now.

Meditation on Outsourcing

I was out of ideas, so I hired a detective.
Call me Gumshoe, he said, but
I wouldn't. Pal, I called him. Alright,
Pal, I said, go see what you can find. A year later
he walked into my office &
slapped me in the face. Nothing,
he said. Then he slapped me
again. Then I paid him.

Warp Drive, or the Cabin Boy of Starfleet

If you've never traveled faster
than light, count yourself
lucky. It does mean things
to the body. Your bones

get soupy, you can't stand up
straight, and you totter
like a baby gazelle, wobbly,
full of fright. But the Captain

with his bald, Shakespearean
grace makes it all look
so easy. The way his big hands
splash across his chest

when he smoothes his uniform
or slaps his combadge
with dictatorial haste. He even
pulls off being pissed

with panache. I, on the other hand,
am only hailed when there's a spill
on the bridge or an accident
on the Holodeck. Too bad,

at this point in history, nobody's
improved on a bucket
and a mop. Swab the deck,
ye dog, he says to me

with a wink, quoting Stevenson,
I think. At night he watches old
Merchant Ivory flicks
or BBC tapes, practicing

his delivery. Make it so, he says,
bare-chested, while I disinfect
his sink. He brushes his fingers
against my cheek and booms,

Don't make me pull rank.
When I slap his hand away,
he laughs. Then he reads a little Pliny
before he falls asleep while I massage

his feet. The second I stop,
of course, he wakes up
coated in sweat. Nightmares
of Romulan attacks or perhaps

it's something deeper
than that, something he can't
remember, or won't. Don't stop,
he tells me, and I don't.

Silver

For Nico

I brought my dead horse
into the field
to graze
between the fat poppies
and burrs.

Bumblebees flew
their propeller planes
right through
his ribs, and his teeth

smashed together
without touching
the dried grasses

when he bent down
to eat. His eyes tossed
back and forth

like snowballs,
watching the sweet gum
sway, the swallows

bicker apart
in the low rows
of soy—the whole world
growing away.

At night the stars
fell down

and burned him
and scared him

into the trees,

where I guess
he's still running,

either toward me
or away from me.

Emergency

I call it the world
but I don't know
what I see.

What do you call
an emergency
that has gone on

for this long?
Do you remember
the operation? (They gave

you a blind spot
so you wouldn't
have to look

at me.) Everything
is an emergency
between you and me.

I point at that part
of the world I know
you cannot see.

The world
is in my blind spot,
you say to me.

I say, it's all
that ever came
between you and me.

Death Star 2

Sometimes science seems like a miracle!
How, when we put our minds to it,

we can build a world-melting laser
on a machine the size of a small moon

that looks, albeit, like something even
bigger and more sinister took a few bites

out of it first—you can still see the jagged spires
of scaffolding and the space-tarps blowing

in the solar wind. But all of this just affirms
my belief that you need a great evil

to get things done: rebels, lawlessness,
untidiness in the provinces. People who don't know

what to do with their freedom and, so,
scarcely deserve it. With people like that

loose in the universe, it's best to strike first
(again), to crush their spirit with the weight

of our great achievements. Unlike them, we get rich
for the right reasons, fighting for order and investment

opportunities, the right to run the cosmos
like a business. Shame not everyone sees it

this way. They destroyed us once. They'd be fools
to think they could do it again.

Note to Super Villain

I don't think I can live
in your secret lair
anymore. The steel blast doors
make me look fat,
and the shark tank
smells like chum
and German cologne
from all the dead
henchmen. You're lucky
they don't start a union.
And the food, salted dolphin
meat and poached sturgeon, lime
juice, coconuts, Siberian gin...
Your harem girls whisper
that your lasers
are just compensation.
And your second-
in-command slaps me
with his beret
for no reason, and shows me
his missing eye whenever
I have a mouthful of food
and you aren't looking.
Sorry about all the gagging.
Sorry I'm no good
with a jetpack
or a spear gun. Sorry I weep
during interrogations.
Still, we had some laughs:
when your cat threw up

on the roulette wheel
in Monte Carlo, or when
we poured sugar
into the gas tanks
of all those MiGs
outside of Minsk.
But most days I wake
up and think, Did
I get my master's
in information science
just for this? Updating
the hit-list archives
and alphabetizing
dead spies? I still remember
your add on Craigslist:
Discreet Multinational Corporation
seeks obsequious technocrat
with anarchist temperament
and blind loyalty
to charismatic tyrant. Love
of travel a must. At first,
I even liked it
when you called us
pets. But I don't want
surgically implanted
gills, or X-ray
contact lenses,
or rocket fingers,
even if they are
state of the art. And
I don't want anyone
to fuck with my heart.

People Need to Talk Less on Planes

Because all they say is
I'm gonna die, I'm gonna die,
or at least that's what I hear
until cocktail number three
when I can finally
enjoy the Captain's sultry whispers
over the loudspeakers, all scratch
and pleasure, and I imagine him
looking pleased up there
in his glittering cockpit,
thinking The sky
is my cologne, or
Hey, those clouds look snappy,
while back here
I watch the flight attendant
blow kisses into the yellow
nozzle of her floatation
thingy and point gingerly
at the doors
that let in the sea
in case of an emergency.
Then I plug in my headset
and watch the in-flight movie
called *We're All Gonna Die*
on the overhead TV
and the actor playing me
is me, and he's pretty good
at sitting very still and then
screaming. I'm not that good
at going 500 mph
and even
worse at dying

that way, and if I ever die
that way, and if you never
get to meet me, just wad this
poem into a ball
that looks like a little white brain
and light it on fire,
and throw it
as hard as you can
off the top of a building.
I'll just be a slash
of flame and smoke
at that point, and if people see it
they'll think what
you think: I was something
terrible happening,
and I was my whole
life, but, God willing, all
you will remember
is the burning.

Teeth Muse

For Kristin

I don't like the little girl
god and her glitters
and wolfsmells.

I don't like the way
she's always sniffling,
drinking rainbow wine

or knocking down barns
with her crutches.

I don't like how she rabbits around
in the bushes
and pops her head out
suddenly with something

in her teeth,
like a dog with a stick.

I don't like: her French
accent, her crayon fangs,

or the black wings, always
flapping, on her flats.

There she is now, peeling
a star, seething.

Her batty eyes all agog.

Making her never-ever-face,
hungry and squinched.

I know

she's just lonely
growing up eternally.

But I don't like
how she threatens

to turn me
into a tree, and carve

a heart in me
around her unspeakable

name. I don't like

how she can only love
one thing at a time.

And I don't like
being this one thing,

being just
this one thing.

Getting Lost on the Back Roads of Pennsylvania, While Trying to Find His Parents' New House, the Author & His Now-Ex-Girlfriend Stop by the Side of the Road & Consider What to Do Next

It is night. I shut my eyes

& they open again.

They are lost
the way a bead

of water gets lost
on a hot mirror.

They itch from the faint
needle fall of stars.

I aim the flashlight
at the map & giant moths
crash into highways

& lakes, like monsters
in Japanese
horror flicks.

My little circle
of light looks

to the tiny
unseen inhabitants

of this paper Pennsylvania

like a tornado
of sun: they burn apart

& tell me to go
home. I am

home, I tell them,
which is why
I am lost. I need their help

getting down
from this ladder
of night & they won't. I need to drive

though the hurt

forest & wind up
at a 24-hour donut shop

where I can sugar myself
& coffee myself

& pretend this country
is not the enemy
of the dawn. Men

live here & ride their snowmobiles
through the soft bodies

of deer. They sharpen their boots
in the mud. They blacken
each other's eyes

with fistfuls of mid-
night. Someone
or something throws a snowball

of midnight at the back
of my head
& the word "fuck"
rolls out the front

which means the map
is broken
& the flashlight

has run out
of ideas. You

are no help. I ask you
to hold the map

& your hands backpedal
into pockets. I ask you
to pour what's left
of the flashlight

into my cupped hands
& the door
sulks suddenly shut.

Inside, we pass the silence
back & forth

like a joint
& take big
selfish breaths

as the headlights flash
into a field,

spotting the flying saucers
of deer eyes
in the grasses.

They are green & lovely
& they mean us no harm.

But when I turn
the ignition, the deer run off
like a gang of hurdlers,
leaving me alone

with you & my fear. Together

we drive past beasts
& night birds
& crackling barns,

seeking the blind
moon. All the small houses

are on strike. The porch lights
haunted with gnats.

& when I roll my window

down to suck in
the dark air, you roll
your window up, as though
there's only so much world

you can take.

Little Matter

I was elected to serve
as your silent official. My job
is to say nothing
once I've finished saying
this one thing. When my term
is up, I will try
to sing and it will go
badly. People will ask me
how my day is going
and I will tell them
about my year. If anyone asks
me what I've learned
I will say that the trick
to preparing for death
is to die a little bit
each day so it doesn't hit you
all at once. Once,
when my father was drunk
he told me, It is up to us
to misunderstand
each other, I think
by mistake. When I am silent
I will be closer to the dead
in an unimportant way,
like taking one step
toward a planet
rising in the night sky.

Dear Things

Persnickety hayricks and grab-assing weeds
dream of unbelief to the pylon birds

and the sieve flowers while my heart walks
its rickety plank into oceans of pollen

and each pitchfork of field tastes good
to the mountains who dedicate their

tonnage and ice to staring contests with
the sky. The mountains nobody me

but I forgive them, while my blimp-headed
father looks down from his heaven

full of frost and love and the cold fireworks
of snow. He sweeps broomfuls of silence

through the trees and I say somebody please
explain these clouds to me please. Somebody

explain these father-eyes and burrs. Now
I'm just a quailburst in the brush, a flailing wing

or three, an agitation of flight; I'm a nothing-
much, a wait-for-me, full of blotched

astonishment and look-at-that. I notice
all the birds and things not noticing me,

but I'm too half brokenhearted not
to notice them back.

Crag

Last night I slipped your photograph
into the *Book of Awe* between the chapter
on floods and the chapter on icy crags
and went to bed early
feeling terribly small
in my fuzzy slippers, feeling
in the dark for my bedside glass of water
like a science teacher
trying to remember
the names of Saturn's sixty moons
thinking if I accomplish this
then I have mastered
the emptiness that surrounds us.
Tomorrow I'll wake up and read
the book's final chapter
on space and I'll place
your photograph facedown
against a page of collapsing stars
and think of you growing heavier
and darker there without me
and calling to me
without sound.

Canteen

I fill it with water
and an hour later
I unscrew the cap

and pour out
dribbles of smoke
and sick wind.
I fill it

with curses and spit
and hand it
to my neighbor
and she says I'm not
falling for that

one again. Then
I plant innumerable

seams of corn
inside the canteen

and come harvest
I twist open
the top and inside
the villagers
are still hungry

and their scythes
are gleaming and sharp.

Dreamburgh, Pennsylvania

For David Blair

Rosy little bridges of goodbye
staple the valley together
over the shaving cut
of this river whose waters
don't make you forget
like that dank rill
in the underworld
but remember odd miraculous
thrills from middle school
like the sound of Velcro
ripping apart when you tore
open your fire-red
Ferrari Trapper Keeper
to pages of notes
about otters the river
cluttered with scows
sailboats barges
and prismatic oil spills
where people catch blind fish
and make a wish
when they throw their empties
in and some days
you think everyone
should wear a bright orange
life vest and bob around
on the water here
in Dreamburgh, Pennsylvania
where the buses are powered
by the collective goodwill
of the people the litter

is beautiful most everyone recycles
and we think about death
only once in a great while.

Notes

"The Awes": Li Po said and did none of the things attributed to him in this poem.

"On the Revolutions of the Heavenly Spheres": one translation of Copernicus's book on heliocentric astronomy, though it's somewhat catchier in Latin: De revolutionibus orbium coelestium.

"Silver": the lines "the stars / fell down/ and burned him," appropriate language from a poem by Nico Alvarado-Greenwood. I use it with his permission.

"Teeth Muse": is inspired by the poetry of Kristin Hatch.

Acknowledgements

The original versions of many poems in Dreamburgh, Pennsylvania have appeared in the following publications: *42milespress.com, Amarillo Bay, The Arava Review, Artifice, At-Large Magazine, Barnstorm, Cider Press Review, elimae, Gander Press Review, H_NGM_N, Hot Metal Bridge, Ilk, InDigest, My Name Is Mud, The National Poetry Review, Paper Darts, Pleiades, Prick of the Spindle, Salamander, Scud, Sixth Finch, SOFTBLOW, Thermos, Third Coast, Transom, Unstuck, Verse Daily,* and *Zoland Poetry.*

About the Author

Gregory Lawless is a graduate of the Iowa Writers' Workshop and the author of *I Thought I Was New Here* (BlazeVOX Books, 2009) and *Far Away* (Red Mountain Poetry Press, 2015). His poems have appeared in *Pleiades, The Journal, Third Coast, The National Poetry Review, Salamander, Verse Daily*, and many others. Originally from Pennsylvania, he lives in Waltham, Massachusetts.